A Tennessee Legend

A

Tennessee Legend

with a
PICTORIAL OF OLD

BOTTLES
& JUGS

Pat Mitchamore

RUTLEDGE HILL PRESS
Nashville, Tennessee

Published in Nashville, Tennessee, by Rutledge Hill Press, Inc., 513 Third Avenue South, Nashville, Tennessee 37210

Design by Bruce Gore, *Gore Studio*
Typography by D&T/Bailey Typesetting, Nashville, Tennessee

Printed in the United States of America

1 2 3 4 5 6 7 8 — 96 95 94 93 92

Introduction

IN EVERY ERA and in every country, legends, which embody a fascinating blend of characters and events, are part of popular history. Some legends may grow in grandeur as each bard, each singer, and each storyteller embroiders new threads into the fabric. Thus they become more fiction than fact. Others have enough basis in history so that historians keep the legend accurate. Whatever the legend entails, it enriches the lives of the hearers.

Tennessee has many legendary characters, but one legend that continually sparks interest is the one from the Cave Spring Hollow where Mr. Jack Daniel first registered his distillery.

The youngest and smallest of his siblings, Mr. Jack Daniel left his father's house early, even by the standards of his day. This developed him into a uniquely independent character, which set him apart from others, even as a child.

Mr. Jack's whiskey has stayed the same for more than one hundred years. And while it is characterized by a unique square bottle, there have been a fascinating array of different bottles in which Jack Daniel's whiskey has been sold.

Mr. Jack, the unique character from the tiny town of Lynchburg, Tennessee (pop. 361), bottled his unique product, Old No. 7 Tennessee Sour Mash Whiskey, in a unique bottle, a square bottle. It is this three-part story—the man, his whiskey, and the bottles which contain it—that has made this legend.

The tradition and romance of legends develop in the retelling of the stories again and again. And so, in the interest of preserving this legend, the story is once again recounted here.

ONCE UPON A TIME, OR
THE LEGEND BEGINS

EVERY STORY has a beginning, and every legend has a starting place. In this case, Jasper Newton Daniel was born to Calaway and Lucinda Daniel in September 1846, their tenth and last child, as Lucinda died five months later.

Jack, as he was called by the family, was a small child. His size—even as an adult he would be only five feet, five inches tall—seemed to necessitate that he develop giant-size character traits. He had spunk and he had gumption, both traits that were admired in his day. These were witnessed early on when, at the age of six, Jack left home to live with neighbors, Uncle Felix Waggoner and his family, because he did not get along with his stepmother. This seemed to be acceptable with everybody because the Waggoners took him in and his father did not retrieve him.

This was a big decision for such a little fellow, but one that started him at this tender age on a course of life and development of character. Jack was industrious and cheerful. He was also quick to learn. His presence in the Wag-

goner household was welcomed and Jack took advantage of the opportunities to learn through the chores that they had him do.

Jack lived for a year with the Waggoners and then at age seven he went to live with Dan Call and his wife, Mary Jane. Dan was just ten years older than Jack and at seventeen was already an accomplished businessman who needed a little helper. He owned a general store, slaves, property, and a still, where he made whiskey that he sold in his store. Dan was also a very good speaker, devoutly religious, and a lay preacher in the Union Lutheran Church.

Although Jack kept in close touch with his brothers and sisters during his lifetime, even living with a sister and her husband for many years, it was these two men who most profoundly influenced his life. Both Uncle Felix and Dan helped to mold and develop the character of little Jack and clear the path that his feet would travel during his lifetime.

Jack was lively and a charming little fellow. He was intelligent and applied himself diligently to every chore that was given him to do. Mary Jane ran the general store and Jack began his life with the Calls by helping her in the store. A store is a good place to learn things like arithmetic by counting money. Reading and writing were necessary, and Jack's penmanship showed an artistic flourish. Flowing and lyrical, his letters would later be prized by ladies who received them. All of these things

Mary Jane taught Jack so that he could run the store. Foremost of all the things that Mary Jane taught, she taught honesty in business dealings. The Calls' religious devotions directly influenced the manner in which they conducted their business and their lives.

Jack began helping Dan at the still about the time he was eight years old. Dan Call had a Negro slave, Uncle Nearest Green, who was the distiller. His two sons, also slaves belonging to Dan, were George and Eli. These two boys were a little older than Jack, and they also helped at the still. It was Uncle Nearest who taught Jack Daniel all he knew about making whiskey, which proved to be considerable.

This, then, was the formal schooling that Jack received in the care of the Calls. Even though Jack was just a little boy and the Calls were charged with his care, Dan paid Jack wages for his work. Jack saved his money until he could buy himself a team of mules and a wagon, and by the time he was ten years old, Jack was buying whiskey from Dan Call which he then sold off his wagon to other country stores in the area.

THE STILL ON LOUSE CREEK

D AN CALL lived in Lincoln County, and whiskey 'stillers in the area made their whiskey in the "Lin-

coln County Way." At this time there were about fourteen
stills in the area, all making whiskey by this process. It
used a sour mash whiskey, a mash using only natural fer-
mentation with no chemicals or other additives to induce
fermenting. Once the whiskey was made, it was filtered
through nine to ten feet of sugar maple charcoal. This
leeching process or filtering mellowed the whiskey and
gave it a distinctive taste.

One reason whiskey was made in this area was the water. The land was rich with limestone springs—a natural,
iron-free water—feeding pools, streams, and creeks.
Spring water is also naturally cold and therefore would
cool the still during the process of whiskey making. Good
water is absolutely necessary for good whiskey.

Aging in those days was a matter of timing. If the
whiskey was not sold right away, it might age for a while
in the barrel. Most often, however, it was sent to the store
and sold within a few days. Production was small, just
enough to meet the demand.

Dan Call's still was set up on Louse Creek, a spring-
fed creek that crossed his property, which he had inher-
ited from an uncle. The Louse Creek still was less than a
mile from his general store. The other thirteen stills in
the area were set up at different spots on the larger Mulberry Creek. Whiskey making was a way of life for these
settlers. Almost every home kept a jug for little celebra-
tions or toddies, and everybody kept some for medicinal
purposes. Since there were no taxes or government con-

trols on the making of whiskey, anybody could make it, and most people did.

Those who didn't make whiskey might grow the corn and grains that the 'stillers used for their mash. All of the grains were raised on farms in the area and the spent mash was used as feed for livestock and hogs. As in modern business, one industry filled the needs of another.

Packaging the product was easy. Whiskey usually went to stores and saloons in a keg or barrel and customers bought it in bulk just as they did their staples of sugar, flour, or meal. They brought their own containers, in this case usually a gallon-size earthen jug. In 1857, a gallon of whiskey cost the handsome price of one dollar. Is it any wonder there were fourteen stills in Lincoln County?

FLAMES OF FURY, WAR, AND LADY LOVE

WHAT BETTER NAME is there for an evangelist than Lady Love? It conjures sweet emotions and puts one in mind of heavenly things, just as she hoped it would. Lady Love, however, was a flame of fire. She came to Lincoln County with heated words against the use, making, and selling of spirits. Like lightning, her fiery preaching against the sins of alcohol struck the conscience of Dan Call. She was the divine instrument to indirectly affect the life of Jack Daniel.

Dan was sincere in his wish to live a devoted life pleasing God and his brothers and sisters in the Union Lutheran Church congregation. Lady Love delivered a thunderous blow to his comfortable lifestyle. Not only was Dan shaken and seared by her words, but so were his wife, Mary Jane, and the entire Lutheran congregation.

This new conviction made a need for great changes in the Calls' business ventures, since Dan both made and sold whiskey. His first thought was he would offer to sell his stilling business to Jack Daniel, a competent distiller. Jack had learned well from Uncle Nearest during the five years he had helped at the still. Also, Jack was a Primitive Baptist and the business would not conflict with the teachings of that church.

Dan offered to sell the still to Jack. Until this time, sales of the whiskey had mostly been to the general store that Dan and Mary Jane owned. But now, the sales there would be stopped also. Jack would need to find other places to sell his whiskey. Jack bought a team of mules and a wagon and began to establish accounts in the surrounding countryside. Using the money he made from the sales to these accounts, along with the money he had saved, Jack Daniel purchased his lifelong business at the age of thirteen.

Lady Love's words had fired change in the young boy's life, and flames of war further inflicted profound effects. The Civil War erupted and the world beneath everyone in the South heaved with tremors. Young men from Lincoln County donned gray uniforms, said goodbye to home and hearth, and set off with their regiments. Dan Call was one of them.

The war produced both positive and negative effects on little Jack's business. On the lookout for new sales markets, he saw Huntsville, Alabama, just thirty-five miles south of Louse Creek, as a natural for his increasing territory. A thriving city, Huntsville was soon occupied by Federal troops. However, the land between where the roads crossed was a rich agricultural area, and therefore a natural hunting ground for troops scavenging for food and produce. Anyone possessing desirable products was at the mercy of foraging soldiers. Business was on the increase, but so was the danger in getting whiskey to market.

Need necessitates best efforts and Jack became a creative marketer.

ALABAMMY BOUND

HUNTSVILLE and the surrounding area in Alabama offered opportunity, and Jack was up to the challenge. Prior to the war there had been ample whiskey and brandy available in this, the state's most populous, county. However, after seven major Union sieges of the city, and the subsequent occupation of Huntsville, the roads were constantly patrolled by both sides: the Confederates looking for deserters and the Federals searching for Confederates. Poachers and bushwackers were all along the backroads.

A little danger seemed to fire the excitement for the young country boy and friends his age. Too young to join the army, they were still eager to see action. Jack had a friend, Button Waggoner, who lived on a nearby farm and was easily talked into joining in the adventure of getting Jack's goods to market.

These boys, Uncle Nearest, and his sons George and Eli filled as many jugs and small kegs as they could get hold of with Jack Daniel's whiskey. The containers were unmarked as there were no government regulations on labeling. Jack was just beginning to sell his product out of his immediate area, and brand identification was unheard of in his neck of the woods.

For this new venture, care was taken to load the wagon to prevent detection of the whiskey by marauding soldiers and road scoundrels. First they placed jugs of whiskey in the wagon close behind the wagon seat. Because side meat was also in demand in Huntsville, it was stuffed between the jugs to serve as cushions. Hay was thickly strewn over the meat and sacks were placed over the hay to hold it down. As Jack and Button traveled the Old Winchester Road toward Alabama, they would stop and pick up old fence rails along the road and throw them on top of the wagon. Thus, they disguised their precious cargo.

When they neared the occupied city, the boys would pull over and wait until midnight to enter the city. They had been told that soldiers would confiscate the whiskey during the daytime. Saloon keepers and store owners purchased their whiskey in the hours after midnight and before dawn. In the daytime the boys went unmolested to grocery and butcher shops to sell their side meat.

A boarding house lady befriended Jack during this period, and he made it a habit to stay with her when they went to Alabama.

These sojourns were dangerous for two young boys. The road traversed a wild and rough segment of the country, and many times they had to break ice to allow the mules to cross a stream. However, Jack made this trip— many times alone—once every two weeks and sold many an unmarked jug of his whiskey in his first effort to market away from Lincoln County.

But then a gentle breeze began to stir in a different hollow.

HOME AND THE CAVE SPRING HOLLOW

IT IS SAID that war makes men out of boys, and it seems with Jack that this was true. The little boy had become a young man. Though still small in stature, he was full of grit and gumption. He had done a big job dur-

ing the war, put away a sum of money, and knew that he could achieve whatever goals he set for himself. Now he made bigger plans for a giant undertaking. And he was less than twenty years old.

Dan Call would be coming back from the war soon, and word had it that he had become even more vehement than before about the evils of alcohol. Although Dan had nothing to do with the operation of the distillery, it was situated on his property. Also, it was difficult to get whiskey to market over hard-rut country roads, and so Jack knew he needed to be closer to the railroad. He planned to increase his production and this required better transportation and a larger still.

Jack found the perfect spot for his distillery. Looking for a location with the good water that was needed, he came upon the Cave Spring Hollow near the little town of Lynchburg, at that time still in Lincoln County although now in Moore County. Lynchburg was only about fifteen miles from the larger town of Tullahoma, where the railroad passed through. According to the young businessman, Cave Spring Hollow added up to the sum of his

needs. He secured the land and proceeded to duplicate the old distillery.

Jack was determined now to grind thirty-three bushels of corn a day, which would increase his yield to seventy-five gallons of whiskey per day. This would take him a while to do. Nevertheless, he made preparation for the increase as he built the new distillery. Jack had to hire some men for his new location, including George and Eli Green, who were now free men.

At the same time Jack moved his distillery, he made a second lifetime decision. Since leaving the Call household, he had been living in a boardinghouse. His sister Elizabeth, or Bette as everyone called her, and her husband, James Conner, a veteran of the Confederate army, had a farm about two miles from the Cave Spring Hollow. They had no children of their own. It was here that Mr. Jack took up residence.

A large two-story house was built in the center of the farm, later to become known as the "Jack Daniel Mansion." It was a beautiful home with a ballroom for dancing. A bachelor, Mr. Jack shared his life with Bette and James here on this farm with a staff of hired help for their fields, grounds, and the house. Many wonderful entertainments and socials were enjoyed by friends and family during the years to follow.

It was the right move for the gentleman distiller, so right that he never changed it. But, other things *were* changing.

THE WINDS OF CHANGE

THE FIRST NIP of biting winds was felt about the time Mr. Jack got his new distillery settled in the Cave Spring Hollow. It was significant of things to come for all southern distilleries. The federal government had started the regulation of spirits during the war, and this was extended to the South after the war was over. Every distiller was required to register with the government, and

This stoneware jug stenciled "Jack Daniel Whiskey Lynchburg, Tenn." dates between 1865 and 1870. It is 15" high, glazed dark brown and sand with an overlapping narrow band of light brown around the shoulder. The maker's imprint indicates it is three-gallon capacity.

a tax was levied in the amount of two dollars on every proof gallon of whiskey produced. This excise tax was collected by the newly established Internal Revenue Bureau. Mr. Jack filled out his papers on his new distillery operation in the Cave Spring Hollow. Dispatching these to Washington, he registered his new Jack Daniel Distillery, Lynchburg, Tennessee. Proud of his venture, little did he realize that more than one hundred years later these papers would make his distillery the oldest registered distillery in the country.

A new still. A new name. And now Mr. Jack showed his pride by labeling the whiskey he made. The barrels and jugs sported stencils showing that they contained Jack Daniel's Whiskey. Mr. Jack had begun to advertise!

A MANNER OF FASHION

AFTER THE WAR soldiers returned home and lives began to be rebuilt. As in all rebuilding, changes— subtle and not-so-subtle—took place. Bushwhackers, vigilantes, and carpetbaggers had their go in rural hills and hollows.

In 1867, Jack Daniel celebrated his twenty-first birthday. He had been on his own for fifteen years, had worked hard, had studied and learned. He had applied himself, saved his money, and invested it in himself. Now he was a

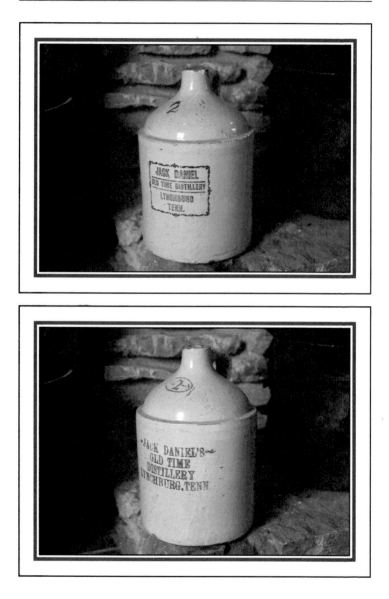

prosperous businessman and his own boss. He had made
friends, from Uncle Felix Waggoner to the slave boys
George and Eli. As free men, they now wanted to work
for him. A graduation of sorts was due young Jack
Daniel. He drew himself up to all five feet, five inches of
his height, swung his 120 pounds onto his wagon, and
headed for the neighboring city of Tullahoma. It was the
booming metropolis of the area, with a railroad bringing
goods from Atlanta and such ports as Charleston and
New Orleans.

Mr. Jack had decided to acquire some uptown style to
celebrate his birthday. When he returned home, it was
with a stylish new formality befitting a young businessman. His shirt was fine linen. He wore a fawn-colored
vest lined with silk. A broad bow tie and a knee-length
tailored frock coat completed the outfit. On his head he
wore a high-rolled planter's hat. From that day on this
was his trademark attire. Each time he ordered new
clothes, it would be the same with only an occasional
change in the fabric, such as silk shirts instead of fine
linen ones.

Age and fashion seemed to be of great importance to

Consistent with Mr. Jack's labeling is the word Old *used in a variety of
ways. Top Jug: Two-gallon jug with cream glaze, stenciled in dark blue: "Jack
Daniel Old Time Distillery Lynchburg, Tenn.", within a square border to re-
semble a printed label, dates c. 1880–1885. Bottom Jug: Another two-gallon jug with the same color glaze and stencil, but worded "Jack Daniel's Old
Time Distillery Lynchburg, Tenn." and without the border, dates earlier
c. 1870–1880.*

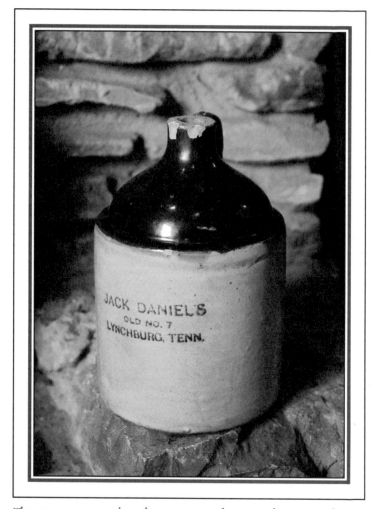

This stoneware jug is about the same size as the jugs in the previous photos, glazed dark brown over cream and stenciled: "Jack Daniel's Old No. 7 Lynchburg, Tenn." from a later period, c. 1890–1895. Mr. Jack began using Old No. 7 as a product name in 1887 and mystery surrounds its origins.

the young man. The words *old* and *fashion* began showing up in various references to his whiskey and his distillery. Jugs and bottles began to display the words "Old Time Distillery," "Old Time Sour Mash," and "Old No. 7" in reference to the whiskey. Old age seemed to suit him well.

BEGINNINGS: A NEW STYLE OF LIFE

AFTER THE WAR everything was growing. The government was developing a stronger, more aggressive, and stable governing organization for the newly reunited country. The new style meant restructure, reorganization, and *regulations*. Some referred to this as *control*. And nowhere was this control more deeply felt than in the spirits industry.

What formerly had been a very simple business of making whiskey and taking it to market now became very complicated. Restrictions were abundant, and these restrictions and laws might be different from one county to the next, causing problems for marketing. The Cave Spring Hollow was in the newly formed Moore County. Tullahoma, where the railroad was, was in Coffee County.

Another law of significance to small distilleries required each barrel, jug, or keg to bear the distiller's name. Labeling was now mandatory. Since Mr. Jack already had begun to stencil his distillery's name on containers, this

didn't have too much effect on him. However, this labeling law demonstrates how the simple life was becoming more sophisticated. Another change was that glass bottles were now both available and affordable. And they were in vogue.

Mr. Jack kept his eye on the competition. His premium whiskey was not to be outdone.

The development of plate-mold inserts in a mold-blown bottle allowed bottles to be personalized with embossments. Therefore, early labels were embossed onto bottles. Each glass manufacturer, however, had his own molds, and so there was much variety in size, shape, and type of labeling in these old bottles, although they were all round. Corks replaced the old corncob stopper, at least until screw caps became available.

Glass bottles were the preferred option. Mr. Jack continued to send his whiskey to market in barrels and jugs, but he also sent along a case or two of glass bottles with

This early glass bottle mold reveals a small embossment at the neck and at the base, leaving a space for a paper label.

corks for the customers' decanting at the retail outlet. This eliminated the problem of breakage during shipment.

There was a negative aspect, however, to this type of bottling. The new federal regulations imposed on distilleries did not apply to retailers. One distiller's whiskey could be decanted into another's bottles. Also, the retail merchant wishing to advertise could provide his own embossed bottle, thereby advertising his establishment instead of the manufacturer of the whiskey. Many times a customer would buy whiskey decanted into a particular distiller's bottle, but upon returning to buy a second bottle of the same brand would receive a different product, although both whiskies were decanted into identical bottles. In spite of the mandatory labeling on the distiller's part, fraudulent sales and abusive misrepresentation to the consumer abounded.

Mr. Jack was now shipping his whiskey regularly to Nashville where his exclusive agent was W.T. & C.D. Gunter. This firm capitalized on the growing fame of Jack Daniel's Old No. 7 by producing bottles embossed with both its name and that of the distillery. The little distiller from the tiny town of Lynchburg was becoming renowned in distant cities and ports. Nashville was a river city, a major stop for riverboat travelers who could take Old No. 7 whiskey to other parts of the country.

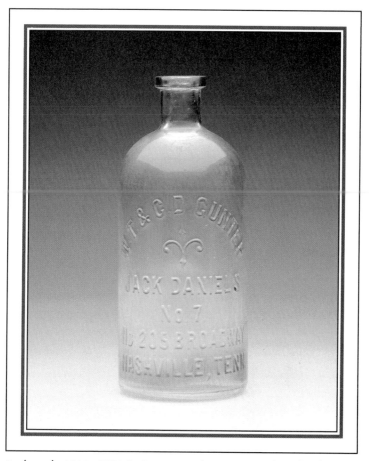

In the early 1890s, W.T. & C.D. Gunter became Mr. Jack's sole sales
agent in Nashville. Capitalizing on the distillery's growing fame for fine
whiskey, it produced stock bottles with its name also embossed on the bottle.
This firm represented Jack Daniel's until the Bone Dry Law was passed in
Tennessee. This was a clear glass round bottle embossed "W.T. & C.D.
Gunter Jack Daniel's No. 7 No. 205 Broadway Nashville, Tenn." Cork
finish, (c. 1895).

RIVERBOATS AND CAPTAINS

WHAT INTRIGUED Jack Daniel about the riverfront sights was the abundance of the carriage trade awaiting passage to far-off places. If Old No. 7 won the approval of these folks, it would add considerably to his product's growing reputation. That's when Mr. Jack resolved to court the favor of riverboat captains.

The most noticeable individual at a river port was the riverboat captain. Dressed in a dramatic uniform, he did not merely participate in river port gatherings, he presided over them. He would tip his hat to the ladies and invite affluent planters and other members of the gentry on board for conversation. These gatherings inevitably led to a sampling of superb cigars and fine whiskey from the captain's private stock. The riverboat captain was a businessman who understood that a steamboat with a fine reputation for accommodations—staterooms, food, and drink—would prosper.

Mr. Jack Daniel knew it, too. That's why he approached the riverboat captain of the *Tennessee Belle* with a most generous proposition. "Sir, I have traveled far and wide selling my fine Tennessee sippin' whiskey and never had less than praiseworthy reports from my customers. It's as fine a potable as you could offer to your personal friends. All I ask is you take one sip. If you like it, I'll see

This bar bottle was created in 1987 to reflect the elegance of the days when steamboats ruled the great waters of our nation. The bell design tapers into a perfectly flat bottom to discourage tipping, a feature the riverboat captains of the era fully appreciated in times of rough waters.

to it that your bottle is filled with Old No. 7 every time you visit Nashville."

Mr. Jack believed that a sip of Tennessee's finest was all it would take to convince the most contrary soul, and once it became the personal choice of the captain, Mr.

Jack knew his Old No. 7 would soon find its way to the steamboat's grand salon, where it would be consumed and appreciated by the carriage trade.

Soon spectators at the Nashville wharf became accustomed to seeing kegs of Old No. 7 along with the mules and roustabouts and bales of cotton and tobacco.

Even when steamboat and paddlewheel travel was in its decline, a visiting riverboat captain might be overheard asking the whereabouts of Mr. Jack Daniel. Whether Mr. Jack was on hand or not, there was always an ample supply of his fine Tennessee sippin' whiskey reserved for the steamboat master. After all, a deal is a deal.

FINE WHISKEY AND TENNESSEE TRADITIONS

TRADITIONS are important in the South, and in Tennessee in particular. Using the Lincoln County process had been the tradition of Mr. Jack Daniel since he began making whiskey. He continued with this painstaking method that Uncle Nearest Green had taught him at Dan Call's still on Louse Creek, and his whiskey was still the finest Tennessee sour mash available anywhere. Many of the other distilleries in the area had changed their procedures, but Jack Daniel continued to distill his whiskey in this time-consuming process. It was a matter of pride. It was a matter of quality. It was his tradition. And he was about to start another tradition.

Mr. Jack had become quite a traveler because, besides being the owner and distiller, he was also the whiskey salesman. While visiting big city markets, he visited concert music halls and theaters. Although Lynchburg was too small to attract anything but traveling medicine shows and one-tent circuses, music was a part of the lives of all the people who lived in Moore County. There were some fine musicians in the area, especially those who could play piano, the fiddle, and other stringed instruments.

The White Rabbit Saloon (c. 1892) Lynchburg, Tennessee.

However, Mr. Jack loved the big brass bands that performed at parades and at concerts in the park. It seemed to him hometown bands were flourishing everywhere but in the tiny town of Lynchburg. People in Lynchburg worked hard and had very little time to go elsewhere to search for culture and entertainment. Mr. Jack thought

In 1972, the Mr. Jack Daniel's Original Silver Cornet Band was faithfully re-created using recollections of the old-timers and this old photograph. The re-created band is today playing the tunes of Mr. Jack's period. Concerts-in-the-park are re-created to crowds of thousands at festivals as far from Lynchburg as California, Vermont, and Washington. Mr. Jack would be pleased to know that both his band and his proud tradition of whiskey-making are preserved as he would have wished. He knew that the demand for quality in music and in whiskey-making were traditions that would stand the test of time.

about this and the seed of a new tradition was planted.

In 1892, Mr. Jack diversified his business and became a saloonkeeper himself, opening two establishments in Lynchburg: the White Rabbit and the Red Dog saloons. He knew that a band would draw big crowds for the saloon openings, possibly even out-of-towners to the Lynchburg town square.

His sense of fun and showmanship was evident as he recruited townsfolk, merchants, and the distillery employees as musicians for the band. He then ordered drums, horns, and other instruments for the players. He loved the sound of cornets and made sure that these were included. He bought all his instruments from the Sears, Roebuck catalog and paid a whopping $277.70 for everything.

The band was an astounding success. For the next twenty years it continued to entertain and delight folks. It played concerts on Saturday evenings and Sunday afternoons as well as for parades, political rallies, and selected funerals.

Later, during World War I, the men of Lynchburg volunteered for service and the band became inactive. It was a loss to the community, but it was not the end of the story.

Mr. Jack was proud of his tradition of whiskey making, preserving the Lincoln County process instead of using easier and simpler methods. He also knew that the demand for quality—whether in making whiskey or in mak-

The Silver Cornet Bottle was inspired by the graceful lines of the featured instrument in Mr. Jack's band. The music of the little cornet was favored by Mr. Jack because its mellow tone reminded him of his most mellow whiskey (c. 1985).

ing music—was such that his traditions would stand the test of time.

Tennesseans love their traditions.

THE BELLES OF LINCOLN COUNTY

M R. JACK DANIEL was country squire, showman, gentleman distiller, and certainly the most eligible bachelor in the county—or in bordering counties, for that matter. Stories abound of the ladies whose hearts fluttered at the mention of his name. His charm was well known and he courted many ladies and corresponded with many more. His beautiful penmanship was put to use wooing ladies in places too far off to visit in an evening.

While Mr. Jack never married, he seldom suffered for want of feminine companionship. Many was the time his shiny buggy clattered through the quiet lanes of Moore County behind his matched and gleaming bays. He drove his team quickly and with a light hand, a man bent on enjoying life and the companionship of attractive passengers.

And who were his fortunate companions? The courtly little bachelor squired most of the eligible women of the area. If he was ever particularly devoted to one, only his closest friends knew. If he were asked about her identity, Mr. Jack would perhaps chuckle slyly and wink. Discretion named no names. The bachelor was a gentleman.

The Belle of Lincoln brand was very popular and was made until prohibition times. This bottle of Belle of Lincoln Whiskey was made after prohibition closed the distillery in Lynchburg and Lem Motlow had moved his operations to St. Louis, Missouri (c. 1912).

Therefore in the early 1890s, when he decided to sell some of his famous whiskey under a new name, whispered speculation buzzed throughout the county. What would be the name of the whiskey? It was the Belle of Lincoln, Straight Whiskey. Each of the courted maidens felt it was she for whom the fine whiskey was named. No one knew for sure because no one could wheedle the secret from Mr. Jack.

In a few years, Mr. Jack deepened the mystery. He designed a special serving decanter, tapering and graceful, with faceted embellishments on its sides. Around the bottom he had his name etched in flowing script. It was called the Belle Bottle. Unlike any other Jack Daniel Whiskey bottle, it looked as though it had been designed by a woman or for a woman. But the discreet gentleman Jack never told who that woman might be.

Very few of these bottles were made and none was sold. Each was given away by Jack Daniel personally. Apparently no records were kept and so today no one knows who made them or who received them.

The Belle of Lincoln brand was discontinued shortly after Mr. Daniel's death in 1911 and the lovely original Belle Bottle is now extinct.

Mr. Jack's Belle of Lincoln label was discontinued shortly after his death in 1911. None of the lovely "Belle" bottles that he produced have evidently survived. This bottle was created from descriptions of old-timers in a 1.75 liter size (c. 1979).

A FORK IN THE ROAD

ANOTHER turning point in the history of Jack Daniel's distillery came in the summer of 1887 when Mr. Jack hired Lem Motlow.

Jack's sister Finetta had married Felix Motlow. They had ten children; the oldest was Lemuel. Lem, as everyone called him, was seventeen when he strode into the Jack Daniel Hollow and asked his Uncle Jack to give him a job. Everyone liked Lem. He was a big youngster, friendly, hard working, and smart. He had just finished his course of studies at Lynchburg Normal Academy, and he needed a job to help his parents financially with the other nine children at home. Jack put Lem to work doing the farm chores around the distillery at a wage of nine dollars per month.

Another young man named Bill Hughes had come to work at the distillery two years earlier. He was regarded as a brilliant scholar in school, had attended a military academy, and was a splendid mathematician. His job at the distillery was handling the still operation. He had a little house not too far from the distillery. Bill and Lem became great friends right off and Lem moved into the little house with Bill until Bill's marriage a few years later.

Bill taught Lem the rudiments of bookkeeping at night and Lem caught on quickly. Lem, it turned out, was as good at mathematics as Bill. In fact, the two were considered near geniuses. Lem could look at a long column of figures with up to four digits each and compute the sum with little more than a glance.

Bill Hughes recommended that Lem be given a job more suitable to his capabilities. After two years at the distillery, Lem was made bookkeeper.

Within the next four years, Lem assumed the duties of manager. He was a natural in the business, just as little Jack had proved to be at Dan Call's still years before. Uncle Jack now had ample opportunity to travel, market his whiskey, and entertain as was fitting for his station in life and the community. He was a natural country squire.

THE CORDIAL HOST AND SOCIETY

M R. JACK had always been a sociable fellow. He was famous for his charm, graciousness, and generosity. In an article printed in the March 6, 1896, edition of the *Nashville American,* the following was written:

> Jack Daniel, who is deservedly the most popular man in his section of the country, enjoys life to its fullest extent. He lives like a prince in one of the finest residences in Moore County, about two miles from Lynchburg. It is fitted up with all the appurtenances for perfect house comfort. The furniture is of the richest and finest to be found, and every-

thing from the cellar to the garret is suggestive of good taste, comfort and luxury.

A magnificent sideboard filled with everything that can be purchased from the foreign and domestic vintages is one of the ideas of life that can be seen in this beautiful home, and Jack Daniel's taste for music and literature are shown in a fine library and an incomparable grand piano. He frequently gives entertainments, in which his friends, and that includes the whole county, are invited and a more generous host cannot be found within the confines of Tennessee.

About his whiskey the newspaper said:

The sale of Jack Daniel's pure old sour mash whiskey is affected only by its quality. The goods are in demand. He has no travelling salesmen and does not need any. His whiskey commends itself. It finds ready purchasers wherever it becomes ready for the market. His widely-known "No. 7" has attained more popularity than any other brand of whiskey that has been on the market in many years. His other popular brand, "Belle of Lincoln," is found on nearly every sideboard and in every retail establishment in the South.

Mr. Jack had many praiseworthy and distinctive qualities, but everyone seemed to agree on his consuming goodwill and generosity. As the *Nashville American* stated, when Mr. Jack entertained, the guest list was not limited to a few.

One such entertainment that became an annual tradition was the First Sunday in May dinners. Involved were the three local Primitive Baptist churches, where his sister Bette, her husband, James, and Jack's brother Wiley

Daniel were members. On the first Sunday in May each year, members of these churches would celebrate the Gathering of the Brethren. Church members, family, and friends would attend. Because one church could not contain the throng, they would all sit outside under the trees, listening and sharing experiences. There would be several sermons during the morning, after which the congregation was invited to dinner at the Jack Daniel Mansion.

Former slaves such as Uncle Ned, Uncle George Felix, Aunt Carolina, and Haley Smith would prepare for the feast for a week. At least a half-dozen fine young shoats, fat lambs, and a veal calf or two would be barbecued in trenches filled with coals. There would also be turkey and chicken baked with dressing and giblet gravy, vegetables of all kinds, pies and cakes, and preserves and jellies. The best of the cakes were baked by Bette herself for the guests.

Upon arrival, gentlemen would be escorted into Mr. Jack's parlor where an array of fine whiskey, brandy, and other potables were displayed. While the ladies prepared for the feast at hand, the gentlemen refreshed themselves with sips from the display.

As soon as the preachers arrived, all would crowd into the parlor where the grand piano stood. Tables were set up inside and out to accommodate all the guests. The first seating would be for newcomers and guests of church members, called "outsiders." The first seating would last about an hour and then the tables would be cleared and reset for the next seating.

This would go on all afternoon until everyone was served. About 4:00 P.M. the Jack Daniel First Sunday in May Dinner would be over. The preachers and a few friends would stay the night and then all would be quiet at the mansion on the creek.

SQUARE AWAY,
99 BUSHELS OF CORN A DAY

WHEN LEM MOTLOW came to work for his Uncle Jack, the distillery was grinding only thirty-five bushels of corn a day, using an old pot still, and the mash was still being stirred by hand in tubs that held about sixty gallons. Lem knew of the advantages in bringing the still operation up to date. "Old No. 7" and "The Belle of Lincoln" were both so popular that all the whiskey was sold as soon as it was ready for market. If production could be increased, then sales would increase.

Lem worked to bring the distillery into a continuous still operation, grinding ninety-nine bushels of corn a day and expanding the warehouse. Although Lem was willing to grind more than the ninety-nine bushels, Uncle Jack was not. He said that to do so would mean the presence of another government storekeep-gauger. In other words, another government officer would be stationed at the dis-

Jack Daniel's now familiar square bottle first appeared in 1895 with the first effort at distillery bottling. Once established, this bottle shape has remained to this day. Originally only available in quart size (above), today square bottles are available in all popular sizes for Jack Daniel's Whiskey. This bottle is clear glass, quart size, and 11" high, with a fluted bowed neck, cork stopper, and embossed with "Old Time Distillery No. 7 [in a circle] Jack Daniel Distiller, Lynchburg, Tenn." (c. 1895).

tillery, and he flat did not want to do that. And so ninety-nine bushels of corn it was.

Bill Hughes, Lem's friend, had moved to Winchester and started his own distillery. Even with the increased production, Lem could take on more work, and so did the bookkeeping for the W.B. Daniel Distillery, which was run by his uncle, Wiley Daniel, and a cousin, Plumb Motlow. When Plumb died, the business was phased out. Wiley also had an interest in a saloon in Lynchburg, which he gave to Lem. Lem continued the operation of the saloon, the first of many successful business ventures for the young man.

Lem's brother Frank was now distiller at the Jack Daniel Distillery. He was a brilliant chemist and was able to increase the production per bushel.

However, in spite of these changes, Uncle Jack was still shipping his whiskey to market in barrels or kegs. Three years before the Spanish-American War, Lem approached his uncle with the idea of bottling their whiskey and maybe even printing their own labels. Uncle Jack had been thinking of doing this himself and the increase in production seemed to mark the right time to initiate such a new idea.

Bottle salesmen were eager to capture this new business at the now-famous Jack Daniel Distillery. Many bottles were presented to the little distiller for his consideration. One bottle, however, caught Mr. Jack's eye. It was distinctive. It was unique. Mr. Jack stood back to look at the variety of bottles before him, and the bottle that was most attractive was squarely in front of him: a square bottle. No other distiller used a square bottle, and no other distiller had a whiskey as fine as Mr. Jack's Old No. 7. Why not choose a bottle as distinctively different as his whiskey?

By the time the bottles arrived in the Jack Daniel Hollow, a carpenter had prepared a cradle to hold a barrel of whiskey. Young Tom Motlow, Lem's younger brother, was out of school for the summer and was helping at the distillery. Two hundred cases with twenty-four square bottles per case were assembled to be filled. Young Tom filled all of these first bottles by himself.

Production was up and a new bottle with bottling operations meant big changes in the Cave Spring Hollow. Lem worked the retail trade for the sales of these first bottles. Demand for Old No. 7 had increased in a number of states, such as Louisiana, Alabama, and Texas. However, Mr. Jack was spurred to expand his public relations further and give the whiskey some grandiose exposure.

In 1896, William Jennings Bryan was the Democratic candidate for president while Robert L. Taylor was running for governor of Tennessee. Bob Taylor was going to campaign for both of them in Fayetteville, just fifteen miles from Lynchburg. Mr. Jack rallied the Lynchburg Silver Cornet Band. New instruments and new drum heads were ordered. Mr. Jack had "Jack Daniel's Old No. 7" printed on each drum head. He also provided a big wagon drawn by a team of fine horses. Mr. Jack, the

The basic square design has remained through the years with minor varia-
tions in the bottle. This early quart bottleneck has less of a curve and is
1/4" longer. Clear glass with cork finish, quart size, 11" high. Embossed
with "Old Time Distillery No. 7 Jack Daniel Distiller Lynchburg, Tenn."
(c. 1895–1900).

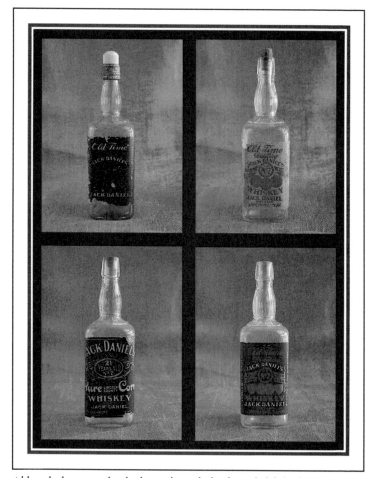

Although the square bottle changed very little, the early labels show changes in color design and content. The twenty-one-year-old whiskey might have been a distilling experiment or a whiskey overlooked in the aging warehouse. It was therefore aged much longer than necessary. It is very rare, but since a label was printed to designate the age, there had to be at least a barrel or more bottled.

band, and others met Bob Taylor in Fayetteville and escorted him to the Lynchburg town square. They made a short stop at Mulberry, where the candidate gave a speech. The band played all the way. It was such a success they continued on to Tullahoma, Shelbyville, and Petersburg.

Advertising was still a simple line; just the name of the whiskey and a statement that the goods were delivered as they were represented. Mr. Jack was a square dealer, sure enough.

THE CENTURY TURNS

WITH THE COMING of the twentieth century, both honors and challenges came to Tennessee's legendary Mr. Jack and his distillery.

For the previous fifty years, Jack Daniel had been building a reputation as an astute, successful businessman of impeccable social standing. His character traits of charm, generosity, kindness, genuineness, and fair dealings were acknowledged and admired. He was known at home and abroad for his fine whiskey, and he still did not have a team of salesmen. His whiskey was known and bought by its word-of-mouth reputation.

Some things had changed. When bottles replaced the original kegs and jugs, Mr. Jack had wisely chosen the square bottle to serve as a distinctive container for his unique whiskey. But one thing had not changed: the whiskey itself and the way it was made. Mr. Jack still distilled his whiskey the time-consuming way he had learned from Uncle Nearest Green. The Lincoln County way— mellowing the whiskey through ten feet of hard maple charcoal—produced a whiskey he could be proud of and which many said was the finest whiskey they had ever tasted.

In 1904 the Louisiana Purchase Exposition, more familiarly known as the St. Louis World's Fair, was held. Large expositions such as this introduced many new

These early labels show the variety of type styles, color, and descriptions Mr. Jack used to depict his whiskey. Those stating "Guaranteed Under the Pure Food Law" date after June 1906.

Men of wealth and distinction could afford to purchase whiskey in large quantity for their home entertaining. Large bottles, however, were a nuisance to carry. Hence, the pocket flask was created. These might be made in silver or other precious metal. They might be elaborately engraved or elegantly simple. The working man, however, was unable to afford such a costly luxury. These pocket-size bottles were referred to as "cheaters." In half-pint size they were an affordable purchase and allowed portability in coat pocket or boot top. About 6" high, flat with cork stopper (later bottles used a screw top) and a variety of old labels.

products and there was to be a judging of the world's finest whiskies. Naturally, Mr. Jack decided to put his whiskey to the test.

The whiskey judging was conducted by a distinguished panel of experts chosen from several nations around the world and headed by a Mr. M. Hoctor, candidate for member of Parliament in Great Britain. It was a very formal affair, with everyone dressed in formal attire. Mr. Jack looked his usual spiffy self in his new frock coat, silk shirt, full bow tie, and high-rolled planter's hat. The little man from Tennessee felt as confident here as he had in his hometown. There was no finer whiskey to be found than his Old No. 7. When the judges completed their deliberations the chairman, Mr. Hoctor, proclaimed, "Gentlemen, the judges have decided that the gold medal for making the finest whiskey in the world goes to the Jack Daniel Distillery of Lynchburg, Tennessee."

It was a great shock to many of the big distillers that a small distillery in Tennessee had captured such a prestigious award, but Mr. Jack was not surprised.

Mr. Hoctor became a great friend of Jack Daniel and in the years to come he encouraged him to enter more competitions to expose his products to the world at large. At his urging, Mr. Jack entered the world competitions in Liège, Belgium (1905). Later, his nephew Lem entered the whiskey in competitions in Ghent, Belgium (1913), and in the Anglo-American Exposition in London (1914). Each time the whiskey won a gold medal.

However, the new century brought an unwelcomed change in social attitudes and traditions for the distillery. The prohibition movement in Tennessee was galloping faster through the hills and hollows than a hound chasing a hare. To some, prohibition meant the elimination of social occasions, but to Mr. Jack it could mean the elimina-

tion of his established business. To his nephew Lem, who now had a wife and a four-year-old son, Reagor, prohibition could mean financial disaster.

Mr. Jack, however, returned to Lynchburg after the St. Louis World's Fair with a victorious spirit. Old No. 7 had just been judged the "world's finest." Mr. Jack had a right to be proud and the smile on his face was as mellow as the whiskey he made.

GIFTS AND COMMEMORATIONS

IN 1896, Tennessee had celebrated the centennial of its statehood with much fanfare and celebration. Visitors flocked to the capital, Nashville, where a gigantic exhibition was held in the new Centennial Park. Big brass bands performed concerts in the park bandshell. Visitors were especially impressed with a full-scale replica of the Parthenon, the temple to the Greek goddess Athena, which exemplified Nashville's claim to be the "Athens of the South."

Mr. Jack decided to commemorate the centennial of his home state with a special Centennial Bottle, which would be as beautiful as the state he loved. He designed a hand-blown bottle with a complex swirled effect on the bottle and the bottleneck which he presented to selected friends and customers, a personal gift to mark this anniversary.

The Centennial Bottle was designed by Jack Daniel in 1896 in commemoration of the centennial of Tennessee's entrance to the Union as the sixteenth state. The bottle is made of clear glass with a spiral design beginning on the neck and continuing down the body of the bottle but broadening at the base. It has a cork finish and is 11" high with black enamel lettering: "Old No. 7 Jack Daniel Lynchburg, Tenn." (c. 1896).

This handsome decanter was designed by Mr. Jack to hold his award-winning Old No. 7 Whiskey. The bottle was tall (11 1/2" high) and slim with vertical fluting in the glass. Since he had won a gold medal, the bands of glass were alternately colored with gold. The handsome lettering was the style of the day with white-on-black embossment (c. 1904).

In 1971 a reproduction of the Gold Medal Bottle was produced in a half-gallon decanter. Although similar to the original, the alternating bands of gold and clear glass were not reproduced. A glass stopper replaced the original cork finish, making the finished decanter 15 1/2" tall, four inches taller than the original. The white-on-black embossed lettering of the period makes this bottle truly distinctive.

Upon his return from St. Louis, Mr. Jack again decided to commemorate a noteworthy event with a special-issue decanter bottle. Winning the gold medal was an outstanding occasion in the life of the distiller, and so he produced a Gold Medal Bottle and presented it as a gift to all those who had helped him to make his fine whiskey.

Noting how popular and prized these special decanters were, Lem Motlow decided to try his hand at designing one also. It became the tool that furthered the fame of Old No. 7 with visitors to Nashville.

All sorts of useful items were used as advertising opportunities at the turn-of-the-century when newspapers were mostly weeklies and magazines were costly and limited. Photo on left shows reproductions now available at the Lynchburg Hardware and General Store. The bottled water (right) was a giveaway to distillery visitors in 1982.

A former Confederate colonel, John Overton, had built a hotel in Nashville and named it the Maxwell House. It was a fashionable establishment, hosting the famous guests that frequented the city. Lem designed a special bottle, more beautiful and shapely than any decanter of its day. He filled it with Jack Daniel Old No. 7 and sent it to Overton, along with a note requesting an interview. Impressed with the bottle, the colonel was even

Mr. Jack Daniel didn't live to see his whiskey win gold medals when it competed in world's fairs at Ghent, Belgium, in 1913, London in 1914, or again in Belgium in 1954. However, his pride in his product and his love for his home state have continued to guide the Tennessee heirs of his historic Lynchburg distillery. In 1982, this bar bottle was commissioned in memory of Mr. Jack's undying affection for the state and the friendly people of Tennessee when a world's fair was held in Knoxville, Tennessee.

more pleased with the whiskey inside and quickly invited Lem to visit him. While they talked, Overton accepted two hundred cases of Jack Daniel's on two conditions: first that the special bottle would be sold only in the Maxwell House and second that Lem would accept co-ownership of the Old Oak Bar at the hotel! Flabbergasted, Lem accepted.

As the reputation of this elegant establishment spread, so did the fame of Jack Daniel Old No. 7. On July 3, 1907, Lem penned this note to his Uncle Jack in Lynchburg:

This photo showing an array of old bottles and jugs features the original Maxwell House Bottle made of clear glass, fluted with traditional triple rings around bottleneck. It was finished with a cut glass stopper and was enamelled in gold. "Jack Daniel's" with "Old No. 7" is embossed in reverse within a gold circle (c. 1907).

Because of the widespread acceptance and interest in the reissue of the Gold Medal Bottle, the distillery introduced a limited number of half-gallon reproductions of the famous old Maxwell House Decanter. Subtle changes differentiate this one from the original. The same delicate lines and fluting as the original are on the glass, but slight changes in lettering and the larger size set it apart (c. 1971).

Here in the Maxwell House it is not uncommon to exchange nods with governors and leaders-of-state. You stand elbow to elbow with generals and tread on the toes of illustrious men. There is a conviviality that defies description. And best of all, they're choosing our whiskey two-to-one over the rest. I think the interesting shape of the bottle may inspire the first drink, but the smooth-sippin' taste does the rest. It is, Uncle Jack, a truly distinctive potable, with special appeal to the educated palate. Incidentally, I have given the name of this majestic hotel to our bottle. Hitherto, it shall be known as the Maxwell House Bottle.

The Maxwell House also contributed to the fame of another beverage. When President Theodore Roosevelt was traveling through Tennessee, he stayed at the elegant hotel. Urged by an aide to rush along, the president replied, "I'm going to finish my coffee. It is good to the last drop." Thus, Roosevelt gave Maxwell House Coffee its popular advertising slogan.

During the president's stay in Nashville in 1907, Mr. Jack heard him speak at the Ryman Auditorium. The Old Lion, Theodore Roosevelt, grinned through his drooping mustache as he spoke to the captivated crowd.

Returning to Lynchburg, Mr. Jack described the particulars of the trip to his nephew and then declared, "Lem, when Mr. Roosevelt runs for re-election next year, we'll send a special bottle to Washington in time for his inaugural!"

Roosevelt had been elected in 1904 by the largest popular vote in U.S. history, but early in 1908 he an-

This Jack Daniel's Inaugural Bottle (c. 1984) was commissioned to honor the 80th anniversary of Theodore Roosevelt's election to the presidency of the United States and to salute the political system that has produced the greatest nation on earth. It is a fitting tribute to Jack Daniel who didn't know much about politics, but knew a good man when he saw one!

nounced that he would not seek another term. This meant the plans for Mr. Jack's Inaugural Bottle would have to be suspended.

Although Mr. Jack did not live to see it, the Old Rough Rider did run again in 1912, and Lem felt an inaugural bottle would be a fitting tribute to Mr. Roosevelt in Uncle Jack's memory. So plans were made for a special bottling of Jack Daniel's Old No. 7 to be sent to Oyster Bay the day of Mr. Roosevelt's victory. But the fickle political winds had changed. Unable to secure the nomination of his own party, Roosevelt ran as a third-party candidate on the Bull Moose ticket and was defeated.

Once again, plans for the Jack Daniel's Inaugural Bottle were laid aside.

SAFELY TEMPERED

EARLY ONE spring morning in 1905 Mr. Jack arrived at his distillery office before anyone else was there. Needing some correspondence that was kept in the safe, he tried the combination, but for one reason or another, the safe did not open. He tried the combination again, and again the safe did not open. A bit frustrated, he gave the safe a good swift kick. He did not hurt the safe, but caused a sharp pain in his left toe.

Soon Mr. Lem arrived and opened the safe for him.

Mr. Jack said nothing about the throbbing in his left toe, partly because he was a little embarrassed at his fit of temper and partly because it pained him to even talk at

Why, I box my goods in tin

Until quite recently custom for my whiskey was simply to satisfied in barrel lots, and earthware jugs. Tough containers able to withstand the shocks of shipment without undue care or worry.

But glass bottles are more fragile. And rough handling though largely unintentional (I am sure) is often commonplace at the many depots along the line between our establishment here at Lynchburg Tennessee, and your sideboard. Hence this novel metal box. The embossed embellishments hereon decorative and colorful though they might be, are to identify the contents within and assure you of the quality, of every drop which I personally stand behind and guarantee your satisfaction.

Jack Daniel Distilly
Lynchburg, Tennessee
Oct. 6, 1906

that moment. The pain did not subside, nor was it going to go away. Six years and six months later Mr. Jack would succumb to complications resulting from the injury.

For a while Mr. Jack was able to carry on in his usual manner, although his spirits were not quite as sprightly nor his wit and humor quite as sharp as they had been. No one noticed until a few weeks later when he began to limp a little. However, when he started using a cane, comments were forthcoming. Mr. Jack brushed them off, noting that a cane added to the look of distinction for a gentleman. By the summer of 1907, however, he was willing to step aside and let someone else oversee the day-to-day worries of the distillery.

He would also let his nephews handle problems caused by the Prohibitionists. A popular ground swell for prohibition was growing not just in Tennessee, but throughout the nation. When Tennessee went dry three years later, in 1910, of the one hundred distilleries which had been operating in the state a decade earlier, only the Jack Daniel Distillery was still making whiskey. In January 1919, the Eighteenth Amendment to the Constitution was ratified, forbidding the making, selling, or transportation of liquor in the United States.

Mr. Jack called a meeting with his two nephews, Lem Motlow and Richard Daniel. "You fellows are up to this fight that is brewing stronger every day against us as distillers," he said. "I'm really not up to this fight. I found a way to stay in business during the war, but this is a different kind of war. You boys are up to the challenge. Lem, you get the papers prepared. I am signing the distillery over to the two of you."

That's all there was to it. Mr. Jack knew that if the distillery had a chance to survive at all in the face of the Prohibitionists, then Lem would be able to figure out how to do it.

Jack Daniel retired to his home where he entertained friends and corresponded with many more. His sister Bette continued to run his household. Among his guests were many ministers of the Primitive Baptist Church. Mr. Jack found solace in their conversations during his increasing confinement.

His condition continued to worsen. Finally, in an attempt to save his life, his leg was amputated. But it was too late, and Mr. Jack died October 9, 1911, at the age of sixty-five.

Newspapers all over the state noted the passing of this famous Tennessean who had befriended many, helped scores, and loved all. Some excerpts from these notices follow:

The *Nashville Banner* (front page story), October 10, 1911:

> Jack Daniel, widely known as a Tennessee distiller, though in recent years he had not been connected with the business, died yesterday afternoon at his home near Lynchburg.
>
> Mr. Daniel had been in failing health for several weeks and his final illness extended over a period of months.

Some years ago, Mr. Daniel joined the Mt. Moriah Church. He leaves a handsome estate.

The *Fayetteville Observer* (an ardent advocate of prohibition, which carried on an aggressive fight against the distilling of spirits), October 12, 1911:

Capt. Jack Daniel died at his residence near Lynchburg Monday afternoon. For the past seven years he has been in failing health and it was known that soon he would reach the river's brink and take passage to the further shore. He was reared in the Primitive Baptist Faith and was a member of that church at the time of his death. The Captain was gifted with superior business qualifications and had accumulated a large estate. He was a pleasant and affable companion and every acquaintance was a warm friend.

The *Lynchburg Falcon,* October 12, 1911:

Mr. Jasper Newton Daniel, better known as Jack Daniel, died at his home near town Monday afternoon after a lingering illness covering a period of at least four years.

A few months ago he went to Nashville and had one of his legs amputated but he never received any relief therefrom. When he had almost reached his majority he began to trade and after he had acquired some means of his own, he went into the business for himself . . . when he purchased the distillery which is now located in Lynchburg. It is said that he ran it 35 years without letting the fire go out, besides building two other distilleries at the same time.

His familiar brand, No. 7, is known the world over and has taken gold medals at expositions in foreign countries. About seven years ago, Mr. Daniel, owing to his bad

health, decided to go out of business but the whiskey still bears the brand name of No. 7. The distillery is now the property of his nephew, Lem Motlow. Mr. Daniel acquired a great fortune, and was always ready with a helping hand for the distressed widows and orphans. He was ever ready to help build schoolhouses and churches, and there are but few that have been built in this county but that have been built with the aid of this man, and they stand as monuments to his memory.

The *Memphis Herald* (editorial):

When the historian of the future comes to write of Tennessee, and reaches Lincoln County, he will probably preface his account with: "It was in that portion of Lincoln which was later to form Moore County that the famous old-time distillery of Jack Daniel was located."

The historian will do this because the excellence of the product of that old-time distillery has done more to give fame to Lincoln County than any other factor or set of factors.

The *Tennessee Democrat,* Chattanooga (editorial):

No more charitable man lived than Jack Daniel. If charity is a cardinal virtue, he was its highest exponent in his section of the state. Many a poor minister of the gospel received donations from him when times were hard.

No worthy charity sought him in vain. He made honest good whiskey, he stood erect among his fellowmen, and despised littleness. A warmer heart never beat in human breast than the one that supplied the life current to Jack Daniel.

These eulogies were written about the man Jack Daniel, a Tennessee legend, after Prohibition had closed all distilleries in the state the year before.

A small man in stature, from a tiny town, Mr. Jack was a *big* person because of the quality of his life and the quality of his whiskey, which exemplified his distinctiveness. From such as this do legends arise.

Postscript

M R. JACK'S NEPHEWS, Lem Motlow and Richard
Daniel, parted as partners prior to Prohibition.
Lem bought out his cousin and continued to run the distillery in Tennessee as long as he could. When state prohibition closed him down, he continued to make Old No.
7 in states that had not yet become "dry."

Just as Uncle Jack had risen to the challenge when the
flames of the Civil War engulfed the South, Lem rose to
another challenge that threatened his very livelihood.

A fearless and energetic man, Lem was likened to a
tireless fire horse. He was also smart. In describing him a
business associate quipped, "He had four or five brains—
and could talk to several people, add a column of figures
as long as your arm in his head, and write checks, all at
the same time."

Lem's hard work paid off. With the advent of prohibition in Tennessee, he relocated his distillery to St. Louis
where production and distribution were still legal. This
was a successful move which added to the growing legend
of Lem Motlow as one of the nation's savviest business-

1991 marked the 125th anniversary of Mr. Jack Daniel's distillery in the Tennessee hills at the Cave Spring Hollow. Every drop of whiskey is still mellowed in Mr. Jack's old-time manner. Jack Daniel's Tennessee Whiskey is the same fine potable that has won gold medals since 1904—unchanged in rareness and taste. This bottle was commissioned to commemorate this anniversary of Mr. Jack and his fine whiskey.

men. He became a member of the St. Louis Merchants Exchange and was considered a great asset to the business community of the city.

He also ran a distillery in Birmingham until Alabama went dry. He then moved his total distilling business to St. Louis.

It was said of Lem that "a man never lived that had a bigger heart than Lem Motlow." During national Prohibition Mr. Lem built up his mule business, and for a while Lynchburg was the mule center of the nation. His auctions continued for a number of years drawing buyers from all over the country.

In 1932 he was elected to the Tennessee House of Representatives and was re-elected in 1934. During this period he initiated legislation that would improve the state's highway system. In 1937 and in 1939 he was elected to the state senate.

The Twenty-first Amendment to the Constitution repealing the Prohibition Amendment was ratified in December 1933. However, this did not affect prohibition laws in individual states. Tennessee had an Anti-Manufacturing Law and a Bone Dry Law. Very few states had all of these "dry" laws before the Volstead Act went into effect. Lem started a drive for the repeal of the state's dry laws.

He lobbied a bill which passed the General Assembly in 1937 which gave him the right to manufacture liquor in Tennessee to be sold outside the state of Tennessee.

This was the first step to fuller legalization.

The legend of Lem Motlow, who continued to work and fight for the rights of distillers during the twenty years of Prohibition, is one as full of drama, hard work, energy, and heart as that of Mr. Jack.

But that's another story.